SUCCESSFUL APPLICATIONS

WORK EXPERIENCE, INTERNSHIPS AND JOBS

POCKET STUDY SKILLS

Bruce Woodcock and Jenny Keaveney

Leabharlanna Poibli Chathair Bhaile Átha Cliath

Du'

D1092730

macmillan
international
HIGHER EDUCATION

RED GLOBE
PRESS

First published 2019 by
RED GLOBE PRESS

Red Globe Press in the UK is an imprint of Springer Nature Limited,
registered in England, company number 785998, of 4 Crinan Street,
London, N1 9XW.

Red Globe Press® is a registered trademark in the United States,
the United Kingdom, Europe and other countries.

ISBN 978–1–352–00489–2 paperback

This book is printed on paper suitable for recycling and made from fully
managed and sustained forest sources. Logging, pulping and manufacturing
processes are expected to conform to the environmental regulations of the
country of origin.

A catalogue record for this book is available from the British Library.

A catalog record for this book is available from the Library of Congress.

Contents

Acknowledgements

A number of people have contributed to this book and we would like to thank them all, in particular the students, graduates and recruiters whose questions and feedback have formed the basis of the advice it gives and our former colleagues at the University of Kent.

We are grateful to Kate Williams and Helen Caunce at Red Globe Press for suggesting this title and for their help and guidance in bringing the book together, and to Sallie Godwin for the illustrations.

What are you looking for?

Whatever your hopes, dreams and ambitions for your future, thinking, researching and planning give them a stronger chance of becoming reality.

A successful application is a journey. Like any major journey, it will be varied, exciting and perhaps unpredictable. You may change your plans or take detours along the way. You will learn new things and gain new insights – not just about the world, but about yourself too. But, before you start this journey, you have a number of choices and decisions to make.

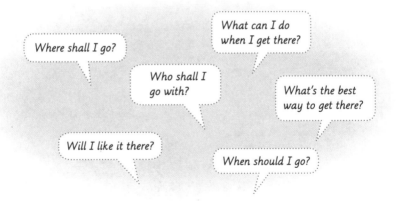

You may feel overwhelmed by all these choices, but don't panic. You can apply many of the skills you are already using in your studies, such as research, analysis, reflection and planning, to find the answers to these questions. This book aims to help you to think about these questions, make your plans and successfully put them into practice.

About this book

In this book, we use the word 'job' to encompass all the different opportunities you might apply for during your time as a student – part-time casual jobs, summer internships, year-in-industry placements, voluntary positions and, in or after your final year, graduate jobs. The same principles underlie all successful applications.

Part 1: You and your goals is about analysing yourself – what you enjoy and what you are good at – and relating this to jobs and careers to find options that are right for you.

Part 2: Developing your job search strategy is about researching jobs and employers, networking, using social media, finding opportunities, action planning and speculative approaches.

Part 3: Successful CVs and cover letters looks at writing and setting out these documents and how to make yours stand out.

Part 4: Successful application forms looks at tackling the different types of questions on application forms.

Part 5: The interview and beyond moves on to what happens after your application has been submitted, from preparing for interviews to coping with rejections.

Successful Applications is set out in the order of the activities you need to do to make your application successful. You may be tempted to jump straight in to the parts on CVs or application forms, but this would be like trying to build a house without first digging the foundations. Thinking about yourself and your goals, and researching jobs and employers, are the essential foundations of a successful application. It's like producing an essay: researching, reflecting and planning before you start to write will lead to a much more successful result.

YOU AND YOUR GOALS

Whatever you are applying for – jobs, placements, internships or voluntary positions – you want something that is right for you. If a position fits with your positive qualities, your skills, interests, personality and ambitions, you'll enjoy it more and get more from it.

Think about:

Reflecting on these questions will help you to find opportunities that will suit your interests, personality and abilities well. This will improve your chances of success.

What makes you who you are?

We all have our strengths and weaknesses, likes and dislikes. Analysing these helps you to make the right choices and apply for them successfully.

What do you enjoy doing?

Do you want a job that interests you? Of course you do! But what makes something interesting for you?

Your interests have already influenced your decisions in life. They have helped you to choose what subjects to study, where to study and what you do in your spare time. You have probably made friends through shared interests. Using these interests in finding careers and jobs will help you to find opportunities you enjoy.

What are your interests?

Use these questions to reflect on what you have done in the past, what you would like to do, given the opportunity, and what you dream of doing. Are there any common themes in your answers?

- What do you like to do in your free time?
- What clubs and societies have you joined at university?
- What courses or modules have you most enjoyed?
- What parts of your work experience have you liked best?
- What achievement has given you the greatest satisfaction?
- What social or political issues most concern you?
- If you could swap places with any three people, who would they be and why?
- If you were to direct a film, what would it be about?
- What is your greatest ambition?

When you are absorbed in an activity, you experience 'flow': a sense of energy and engagement, when time flies by and nothing outside what you are doing can distract you.

The figure on the next page shows six broad groupings relating people and work environments, developed by American psychologist John Holland (1997).

Realistic
The Doers
Like practical activities with tangible results such as making or fixing things

Conventional
The Organisers
Managing information, collecting, computing

Investigative
The Thinkers
Research, analysing, working out problems

Interest themes

Enterprising
The Persuaders
Influencing, leading, directing, selling

Artistic
The Creators
Designing, writing, performing

Social
The Helpers
Supporting, assisting, advising, teaching

Finding a role that corresponds to your group is a good recipe for being able to use your interests in your career.

Imagine you are walking into a room where people from each of the above six groups are already interacting. From the brief descriptions of each group, which three groups do you feel you would be most drawn to? Note them below in order of preference.

Group 1	
Group 2	
Group 3	

Your interests may well overlap two or three groups. For example, an architect may be artistic and investigative, while a financial adviser could be enterprising, conventional and social.

For more about Holland's groups, and a free online test, see www.123test.com/holland-codes-career-tests

Finding roles and organisations that use your interests, and the strengths and skills they have helped you to develop, will enable you to get the same kind of 'flow' in your work that you do from your interests.

What kind of person are you?

Your personality can strongly influence your career choice. **Outgoing** and **independent** people may enjoy a sales career but get bored in laboratory research. A police officer has to be **resilient**, as does a TV producer, or anybody who commutes! **Tact** and **sensitivity** are important for helping careers, such as social work, but also help you get on with colleagues.

Look at the figure, and note your three strongest personality traits. For each of the three, give examples of where you've used it. These traits could provide useful material for your application form or CV profile.

Personality trait	Example of where you've used it

What skills do you have?

'Skills' means more than practical skills such as IT or languages. It also means general aptitudes, known as 'transferable' or 'soft' skills. These aptitudes are of interest to all kinds of employers.

Look at the following diagram of skills needed in different jobs and write down those you think you are good at, or most enjoy using.

	Report writing	
Accepting responsibility	Enthusiasm	Summarising	Listening/empathy
Attention to quality	Commercial awareness	Editing	Telephone skills

Being assertive

In writing   **One to one**

Presenting

Learning new skills   **Professionalism**   **Communicating**

Giving/accepting constructive criticism

Using initiative

Creativity   **SKILLS**   **Cooperating**

Lateral thinking   **Problem Solving**   **Organising**

Negotiating

Data handling

Persuading

Time Management   **Leading**

Motivating

Analysing	Evaluating options	Prioritising	Decision making	Driving results	Delegating
		Action planning			
Investigating	Working to deadlines	Adaptability	Setting objectives	Determination and resilience	

You probably already have many of these aptitudes, even if you may need to develop them, or add new skills, before you can apply for some jobs. Your studies, part-time jobs and extracurricular activities will all have helped you to gain new abilities, maybe without realising it!

Your skills are often reflected in your interests. If you are good at something, you are likely to enjoy it and seek out opportunities for doing it. This practice helps you to improve your skills still further and get even more enjoyment out of the activity.

Work on developing skills that are important for the career you want, especially any you feel you are weak in. Some of the things you may need to work on, such as computing skills, can be resolved by practical training – your university may offer this. Others, such as persuading, are best improved by practice, through work experience or other activities.

How to develop yourself at university

Activity	Abilities you could gain
Completing a group project for your course	*Teamwork, planning*
Producing a report	*Writing, analysing information*
Marketing a student society	*Writing, social media, persuading*
Helping to run an event	*Organising, teamwork*
Becoming a student mentor	*Listening, motivating*
Being a course representative	*Spoken communication, negotiating*
Being a student ambassador	*Persuading, presentation skills*
Writing for the university newspaper	*Writing, creativity*
Standing for election to a committee post	*Persuading, confidence*
Sharing tasks while working in a restaurant	*Teamwork, adaptability*
Helping a dissatisfied customer in a shop job	*Problem solving, listening*
Volunteering at an environmental clean-up	*Helping, teamwork*
Coaching junior players in a sports team	*Leadership, motivating*
Working on the lighting system for a play	*Teamwork, problem solving*
Working in a part-time job while studying	*Time management, adaptability*

How do you like to work?

Evaluating the way you prefer to work is important in helping you choose the right job role and find an organisation where you will thrive.

Do you prefer to work **A ☐ independently or** **B ☐ in a group?**	*Students who work well in teams should prosper in organisations that stress cooperation but may dislike highly competitive environments*
Do you like to **A ☐ take the initiative or** **B ☐ follow set procedures?**	*Students who like to take the initiative will enjoy working in companies that stress empowerment and personal accountability but feel frustrated in situations where they are required to follow precise procedures*
Do you work best **A ☐ under the pressure of** **deadlines or** **B ☐ do you like to plan ahead?**	*Students who work best under pressure will thrive in environments with lots of targets and deadlines*

Thinking about your preferred working style, and finding employers that value and support people who work in that way, helps you to find job satisfaction. Part 2 looks at researching employers to find those that best fit your personality, interests and working style.

There are many factors that go into making career decisions. Analysing your skills, interests and personality gives you a focus for choosing the right career. You can then plan how best to achieve this.

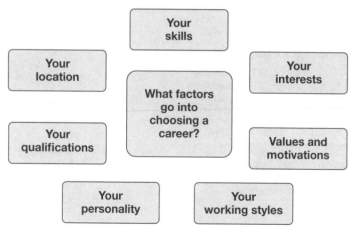

Now let's put some of the above together, using the exercises you did in Chapter 1, to see which factors may be important in your own career choice.

When choosing my career	
Which **skills** would I most like to use?	
What **interests** do I have that might be relevant?	
What **personality traits** do I have that might fit the careers I'm considering?	
What **working styles** would I prefer to adopt?	
Have I particular **values** that would be important (for example, money, helping others, work–life balance, security)?	
Do I want to use my **degree subject** directly in my work?	
Does **location** matter? For example, if you are a mature student with children in school, you may not wish to relocate	

The Career Planner section of the Prospects website (www.prospects.ac.uk/planner) will help you to match your skills and personality to over 400 job profiles and gain detailed information about these jobs. Programs like this can't guarantee to find you your perfect job, but they can help you to focus your ideas if you don't know which job areas to aim for.

Reflective writing in this series has a chapter on 'Reflection for career planning', which helps you to use the analytical and writing skills you need in your studies for career planning and making applications.

Setting goals

Your job search will be less stressful if you have a clear direction. Setting goals and writing a plan at the start of your job search has a big impact on success (Turban et al. 2009).

Action planning

An action plan helps you work out:

What your goals are

How you can achieve them

What steps you need to take

Your goals should be **SMART**

S	**Specific:** clear and unambiguous
M	**Measurable:** how will you know that you have reached your goal?
A	**Achievable:** your aim must be realistic, not a fantasy
R	**Relevant:** it must have real value and importance to you
T	**Time bound:** you need a clear idea of when you expect to reach your goal

Without these SMART objectives, a plan is just a dream.

But setting SMART goals and devising a strong action plan can turn a dream into reality. First, set your goal and assess it against the SMART criteria.

S	What's my goal?	*To become a broadcast journalist specialising in politics*	Unlike 'I want to work in the media', this is a **specific** goal – there are many job roles in media!
M	How will I know when I've achieved it?	*By getting an offer of a job!*	
A	How achievable is it?	*This is a highly competitive field and I won't be able to get my dream job straight from university – I will need to plan a series of intermediate steps to reach this goal*	Be realistic – but if your goal is not immediately achievable, this doesn't make it unachievable
R	Why is this goal important to me?	*Because it fits with my interest in politics and my enjoyment of writing and presenting*	Hard goals need to be important to keep you focused and motivated
T	What timescale shall I work to?	*This is a long-term goal and I realise it could take some years to reach it*	

A long-term goal will need to be broken down into many small steps and you should review your progress regularly

After this, break your plan down into steps. Think of all the things you could do to take you closer to achieving your goal. Break down any large steps into smaller components, so that your goal doesn't seem so difficult to achieve.

List detailed and specific steps

Break these steps down into individual and manageable tasks

Stick to your dates – you could reward yourself with a small treat each time you complete a step!

Do this regularly and make changes if needed. Have a back-up plan

MY OBJECTIVE IS: To become a broadcast journalist specialising in politics TO ACHIEVE THIS, I NEED TO:	Target date for completing this step
Step 1: Gain experience in journalism	
Step 1a: Contact the student radio station to find out what opportunities they offer	
Step 1b: Visit the careers service for feedback on my CV and advice on approaching employers	
Step 1c: Contact the alumni office and search LinkedIn to find out whether any past graduates from my uni are working in this field	
Step 1d: Research these graduates and prepare a personal email to get in touch with each one of them	
Step 1e: Research local radio and television stations to see whether they offer any opportunities for work experience	
Step 2: Review my progress and decide on my next steps	

Write down your goals and plans. Writing your goals on paper has an almost magical effect, helping you to commit to that goal. Stick it on your wall to keep your focus visible.

You should now have a clearer idea of what you want from your career and what you have to offer employers. This will help you to find opportunities to apply for jobs that fit with this.

Part 1 was about you and what you want. Part 2 is about using research and networking to find out what employers want.

Taking some time to research employers before you start to make applications helps you to:

▶ Find out what employers want from candidates
▶ Decide which employers interest you
▶ Tailor your application form or CV and cover letter to that employer
▶ Show your motivation and knowledge
▶ Answer the key question: 'Why do you want to work for us?'
▶ Feel confident at interview
▶ Find a position that is right for you!

Six strategic questions to ask about employers

These questions are the foundation of your research:

What does the organisation do? **What** products does it make? **What** services does it provide? **What** roles does it recruit into? **What** does it look for in candidates?
Who are its clients? **Who** owns it? **Who** does it own? **Who** are its competitors?
How is it structured and managed? **How** does it fit your career plans and goals?
Where is the head office? **Where** are other offices or operations located? **Where** would you be working?
When have things changed or when might they change in future? Have any significant events (such as mergers or takeover bids, changes in senior management or new product lines) taken place recently? Are there any current events (such as new laws or trade agreements) that may affect its business?
Why do you want to work for this organisation? Would it fit your work style and values?

You can find the answers to these questions from organisations' own resources, general careers sites, news/business media, social media and your own networks.

Networking: building networks and using them for research

Networking is one of the most useful ways to research jobs and careers. It isn't about pushing yourself in front of people and giving them a sales pitch. Networking is about connecting with people who can share their knowledge, answer your questions and help you find out what a job or career area involves. If you then decide that you want to work, or gain experience, in this area, your network contacts can give you tips on job hunting and what recruiters look for.

Most people enjoy talking about their work and are usually happy to help others who are interested in that work. Who do you already know? Who else could help you to make contacts in your field of interest? There may be more people out there than you think.

Building your network

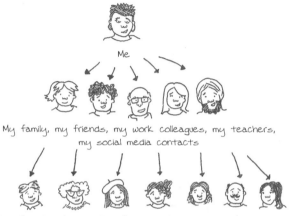

Me

My family, my friends, my work colleagues, my teachers, my social media contacts

Their family, their friends, their work colleagues, their teachers, their social media contacts

Opportunities to meet and network with people in your field of interest could also come at careers fairs, talks and other careers events or at academic and professional conferences. Your university may be able to put you in touch with past graduates.

Keep alert for unexpected networking opportunities. Anyone you meet (in the pub, on a train, at the gym) could become part of your network!

'I wanted to get into speech therapy but didn't know anybody I could get advice from. Then one day my mum mentioned this to somebody at work and it turned out his daughter was a speech therapist! She agreed to meet up with me for a chat and I learned so much from her about the work and what I would need to do to get into it. Now I'm volunteering with a group for young people with brain injuries and have arranged a placement at a special needs school for next year.'

Social media networking

Networking doesn't have to be face to face. Social media platforms are great resources for exploring organisations and job roles, finding people working in them and making contacts.

Key social media sites for networking

LinkedIn	Twitter	Facebook	Blogs	YouTube
Network with professionals from different career sectors, regions and institutions	Follow people or companies and join in conversations	Companies and professional bodies use Facebook too!	Writing a blog can show your writing skills, professional knowledge and enthusiasm	Promote yourself and your creative skills on video

For most students and graduates, LinkedIn is the key resource for professional networking. Joining LinkedIn while you are still a student will help you to find work experience, develop your contacts network, join groups of people who share your interests and build a professional online profile that will help you to find opportunities.

Creating your LinkedIn profile

A LinkedIn profile is like an online CV, but can include more information and more types of information, such as recommendations from previous employers and other connections.

Your profile picture, headline and summary make up your 'introduction card'. They are the first things that potential contacts will see of you on LinkedIn, so make sure that they give a positive impression of you.

Use a head-and-shoulders photo for your profile picture. Wear smart clothes and smile!

The headline says who you are, what you are doing now and what you are looking for. For example, 'Final-year Sports Science student at the University of Trafford seeking opportunities in sports management'.

The summary section is where you can outline your key experience, interests, skills, career goals and achievements. Keep your summary to around 150 words, such as:

> I have strong organisational and motivational skills and a keen interest in the sports business. I promoted the Trafford Tigers men's hockey club on campus, ran taster and coaching sessions and captained the first team throughout an unbeaten season last year.

After this, you can set out your experience, education and skills as you would on your CV – Part 3 shows you how to do this.

A valuable feature of LinkedIn is that you can ask people you have worked or volunteered with to endorse your skills or write a recommendation for you, providing support for what you say about yourself.

The more connections you make, the wider your network. Your connections could be fellow students, work colleagues, tutors or employers.

Keep your profile up to date so that you are always prepared for new networking or job opportunities.

The University of Birmingham's 'LinkedIn Guide for Students, by Students' (www.birmingham.ac.uk/Documents/alumni/graduatecareers/linkedin-guide.pdf) is an excellent guide to creating a good profile and making the most of LinkedIn.

Check your online presence – employers will!

Surveys show that 70% of employers check candidates' social networking sites before interview (Salm, 2017), and almost half say that they have rejected applicants because of what they have found there.

The most common reasons employers rejected a candidate based on their online presence	
Inappropriate photographs, videos or information	39%
Posts about alcohol or drug use	38%
Discriminatory comments related to race, gender, religion	32%
Negative comments about previous employers or fellow employees	30%

Social media can work for you in a positive way too.

Reasons employers hired a candidate based on their social networking site	
Candidate's background information supported their qualifications	38%
Showed great communication skills	37%
Presented a professional image	36%
Showed creativity	35%

What would an employer find if they searched for you?

Start your social network check-up by Googling your name. What could an employer discover about you if they did this? Check images too!

Positive things about you on Google	Negative things about you on Google

Next, check Facebook, Twitter and other social networking sites you use regularly.

Ask yourself	Facebook	Twitter	Other
Would I be willing to read out my last five status updates in an interview?			
What impression would my profile picture give to an employer?			
Have I said anything that might be seen as offensive? Do any photographs show things I wouldn't want an employer to see?			
Have I said anything negative about my work, studies or other people?			
What groups am I a member of?			
What posts have I liked or commented on?			
Do these sites show anything of my skills and experience?			
What changes (if any) should I make to my online presence as a result of this audit?			

Tips for protecting your online reputation:

▶ If you follow companies and professional individuals on social media, it can be useful to set up a dedicated account for this purpose – one which won't get mixed up with your social life.

▶ Set your privacy settings to a high level so that only friends can see your posts and photos.

▶ If you are on LinkedIn, use it actively. An out-of-date profile, or one with hardly any information, will be frustrating for anyone who looks at it and it won't show the skills and professionalism that employers look for.

Networking successfully

Whether online or face to face, networking is a chance to build a relationship with someone who is willing to help you. Don't just focus on what you can get from your networking contacts. Effective networkers show a genuine interest in others, ask questions, listen to the answers and build on those answers to move the conversation forward.

Before you make contact, do some online research to gain basic information about jobs and careers. Then decide what else you want to find out and plan the questions you are going to ask.

Always thank people afterwards and let them know what steps you are taking to follow up on your contact with them. If appropriate, you could endorse or recommend them on LinkedIn for the help or advice they have given you.

The University of Kent online booklet, *The creative career search*, has much more advice on how to network effectively.

Once you have developed your networking techniques and begun to build up contacts, you can use them to find positions that may not be advertised, or to approach potential employers to ask about possible opportunities. This is called 'creative job hunting' and is covered in Chapter 5.

4 Find the right match: analysing opportunities

Applying for a job, placement or internship is a matching process. Is it the right position for you and are you the right person for this position? The more you can find out about jobs and careers, the better the match will be.

Recruitment advertisements are often the start of this matching process. They aim to give enough information about what the post involves, and what the employer is looking for in candidates, to attract potentially good candidates. This saves both sides from wasting their time on inappropriate applications.

Scanning vacancy sites is a good way to begin your job search. It gives you a wide range of options and shows you employers who are actively recruiting. Job sites that focus on students and graduates (such as Prospects and TARGETjobs) will save you having to sift out lots of vacancies that require more experience than you have to offer at this stage. LinkedIn also carries job vacancies, which can be targeted on your career interests.

Large organisations usually have a set recruitment cycle. The application process for smaller companies is often much shorter and recruitment may take place at any time of the year.

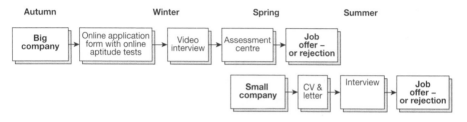

The job profiles mentioned in Chapter 2 include links to employers and relevant job sites.

Not all employers advertise, however, especially smaller employers, or employers in highly specialised areas of work. Networking and speculative applications can help you to discover these opportunities.

Analysing job advertisements

Job advertisements normally set out:

▶ What the job involves – the **job description (JD)**
▶ What they are looking for in candidates – the **person specification (PS)**.

This helps you to assess whether you **would want to apply** (does the JD sound interesting?) and **could apply** (how well do you match the PS?).

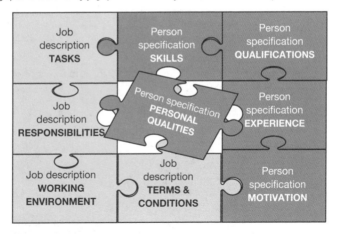

The JD and PS may be linked from a job ad or included in the ad itself. Job descriptions and person specifications linked as separate documents are likely to be very detailed, but those that form part of the ad may be much briefer.

This information will help you to think about what the employer wants to see in your application and select the most relevant parts of your experience.

Only a limited amount of information can be included in the JD and PS. It's still essential to research the employer, using their website or other resources (see p. 142). Doing this research will help you to answer motivational questions (see Chapter 9).

Meeting the person specification

The person specification is the employer's wish list. It sets out the skills, qualities and experience they want. Some of these may be marked as 'essential' and some as 'desirable'.

Experience and knowledge	Essential	Desirable
Experience of working to deadlines and prioritising competing demands	✓	
Experience of working in a customer service environment		✓
Knowledge of MS Office, particularly Excel	✓	
Skills and abilities		
Good team player	✓	
Numerate	✓	
Motivated and enthusiastic	✓	
Confident, with good people skills	✓	
Good written communication skills	✓	

A successful application matches the qualities, skills and experience that you have to offer against those on the employer's wish list.

Look at this brief JD (the responsibilities) and PS (the skills required) and think about what the employer wants.

HR graduate trainee

Enthusiastic and very organised graduate to support our HR team with day-to-day administrative tasks as well as HR activities such as recruitment, staff engagement and retention.

Responsibilities

- Liaising with managers and recruitment agencies to coordinate recruitment activity
- Maintaining a range of employee data and assisting with analysis and reporting
- Assisting with administrative duties, other tasks and ad-hoc projects.

Skills required

- Professional attitude with excellent written and verbal communication skills
- Able to prioritise tasks and meet strict deadlines while working under pressure
- Strong team player able to work within a team at all levels
- Excellent attention to detail with strong analytical and administration skills
- Good knowledge of Microsoft Office applications, in particular Excel.

This PS gives lots of clues as to what a successful application should include.

- Teams you have worked in
- Times when you have organised yourself or other people
- Times when you have worked accurately under pressure and to deadlines
- Times when you have communicated with other people, verbally or in writing
- Your willingness to carry out a variety of different tasks
- Your enthusiasm for this role.

Your skills and personal qualities	How you can demonstrate these	
I have a professional attitude	I have worked in customer-facing environments and taken on responsibility	Did they volunteer to take on extra responsibility or were they chosen? Either way, that's good
I am well organised	I have supervised other people and planned activities	Can organise others as well as themselves
I can work under pressure	I have worked in busy retail environments	
I can manage my time and meet deadlines	I have managed my work, study and extracurricular activities and never missed an essay deadline	
I work well in teams	I have worked in teams on course projects, at work and as a volunteer	A good mix of different teams and types of people
I have good analytical skills	I have managed information for essays and projects	
I am competent in using spreadsheets	I took a short course in Excel to help with my assignments	Shows motivation

Find a job ad that interests you and analyse the job description and person specification as in the example above. Think about:

What does the work really involve?

Could I do it well?

Why does this job interest me?

How could I prove this?

Would I enjoy it?

If not, what would I have to do to meet their requirements?

Do I have what they are looking for?

Find the right match: analysing opportunities

Be realistic but positive: you don't always need to fit every single point in the JD and PS. At the start of your career, it isn't always what you have already done, but what you can show you are capable of doing.

For more on person specifications and how to meet them, see *Reflective writing*, Chapter 17, in this series.

What if you really don't feel able to apply at this time?

The JD and PS may include specific items that you don't feel competent in at this stage. These may be practical requirements ('Full clean driving licence' or 'Fluent in French') or seek a level of experience you can't yet offer.

Don't be discouraged if jobs that appeal to you seem out of reach. Job ads do more than just promote current vacancies: they also tell you what jobs involve. Analyse them to get an idea of what the jobs you would like to do require. Think how you might be able to meet these requirements in future. Do you need to build up experience in other job roles, or gain further qualifications? LinkedIn profiles are a good way to find out how people doing your dream job got there.

Action planning for job applications

You can use the action planning techniques covered in Part 1 to structure your job applications too.

MY OBJECTIVE IS: To gain a year-in-industry placement at BigCo TO ACHIEVE THIS, I NEED TO:	Target date for completing this step
Register on the company website to access their application form	1 November
Read through the form and gain an understanding of the questions	2 November
Look at the company's undergraduate recruitment pages to check what they look for, what the placement scheme offers and what the closing date is	3 November
Check with my placement officer to see if any final-year students or recent graduates from my department have done a placement at this company in the past, and whether I would be able to ask them about their experiences	4 November

Different employers ask similar questions in different ways, so be alert

Research background to the company using their website and other resources	5 November	Use the whole site, not just the information for students
Think about examples I can use to show my skills and competencies on the application form and select the best ones to use	6 November	
Draft out the application form in Word	9 November	Take time between these stages
Review my answers, make any necessary amendments and complete the online form	12 November	
Review the online form to double-check	13 November	Try not to do this on the closing date itself! Early applications are more likely to succeed
Submit my application	14 November	

This planning and research are key to a successful application. Finding out about the job and the employer will help you to be sure that the position is right for you. Using this knowledge in your application will help you to stand out from other candidates.

This all takes time, which may be difficult to fit in with your studies, but the effort you put in will pay off.

'A candidate who has made an effort to learn about my business and adapt their CV and cover letter to show clearly that they have what I'm looking for has already demonstrated that they can research, analyse and write persuasively and are potentially a good employee.'

(Head of PR agency)

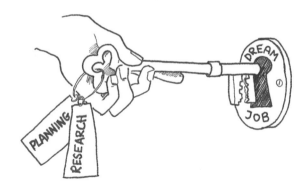

As mentioned above, contacting employers directly to ask if they have any opportunities for you (a 'speculative application') can help you to find opportunities that aren't advertised.

This is part of 'creative job hunting' – using your knowledge and networks to put yourself over directly to employers. This gives you control of your job search: rather than wait for jobs to be advertised, you can make the first approach and sell yourself to recruiters.

Creative job hunting only works if you research opportunities, develop your networks and target organisations carefully. Your experience of networking to gather information will help to prepare you for making these direct approaches.

Ways of approaching potential employers

Method	Advantages	Disadvantages	Tips
CV and cover letter	Gives the employer plenty of information about you, which can be read at a time that suits them	Popular employers get many speculative CVs	Keep your CV concise (one page only) and target it carefully
Phone	You can talk directly to the employer and answer any questions they have	Getting through to the right person may not be easy	Call early in the day, when they may be less busy. Plan what you are going to say to them.
Face to face	You can make an impression in person	Depending where you meet, the employer may not have much time to talk	Don't be pushy. Offer to follow up with a phone call or email
Social media	You can target and personalise your approach. Employers can easily access your own profile if they are interested	Again, standing out from the crowd can be challenging	Don't ask for a job in your very first contact. Ask for advice or comment on their posts and build your contact this way before you ask about jobs

Whichever approach you use, you must be able to give a personal reason for your interest in that employer and show them why they should be interested in you.

Why that organisation?

How did you hear about them and what interests you about them?

I talked to one of your graduates at the careers fair and was impressed by how much input they had into projects …

I use your blog to keep up with developments in the industry …

I watched your CEO's TED talk on cybersecurity …

What can you offer?

For my second-year project, I …

During my work experience placement, I researched …

I took part in a 24-hour university hackathon …

The 'elevator pitch'

Imagine that you arrive for a networking event that is being held at the top of a skyscraper. As you get into the elevator (lift in the UK), you are joined by the top boss of the organisation and the two of you will have a minute alone together before the lift reaches the top floor. You have a unique opportunity to introduce yourself, tell the boss something about you and make an impression on them. If you have had the foresight to prepare a mini-statement about yourself, you won't be stuck for words and can make the most of the opportunity.

OK, so you may never find yourself in this actual situation but this strategy can be used in any short meeting, such as a careers fair, in a phone call, or at a networking event. It's rather like your CV profile, so the examples in Chapter 6 will help you to create an effective elevator pitch. You could also think of questions you would want to ask the employer.

Being extra creative

Some job seekers have succeeded by using highly original and creative approaches.

> *After many unsuccessful applications for investment banking, a graduate printed 100 postcard-sized CVs and placed one on the windscreen of every expensive car he came across in the financial centre of London. Next day, he got several invitations to interviews.*

> *An unemployed graduate walked around his town centre wearing a sandwich board asking for work experience. A local company was impressed with his initiative and offered him a placement, which quickly led to a trainee management role.*

Copying these approaches won't necessarily work for you – they are no longer fresh or original – but their stories may inspire you to devise your own extra creative campaign. There are no limits to creative approaches to finding jobs or experience.

SUCCESSFUL CVs AND COVER LETTERS

You're now ready to make your application – to tell employers about yourself and what you have to offer.

This part looks at CVs and cover letters: what they are, what to put in them, how to set them out and how to use them to persuade employers that you are right for the job.

Together, a CV and cover letter make up a marketing document that shows your unique set of skills and attributes and relates these to the employer and the position you want.

There is no 'one best way' to set out a CV. It is your document, it is all about you and although there are some 'building blocks' that most employers will expect to see in it, you can arrange them in the way that markets you most effectively.

The building blocks of a CV

PERSONAL DETAILS	
Your name and contact details	

EDUCATION	WORK EXPERIENCE
Your degree and secondary school studies	Any full- or part-time experience, paid or voluntary

SKILLS	INTERESTS
These may be practical and/or transferable skills relevant to the job you are applying for	Your hobbies and extracurricular activities. You can include 'achievements' here

These building blocks can be arranged in various ways, so think about which would best showcase what you have to offer, highlight your strengths and minimise any weaknesses.

Let's look now at the main building blocks in more detail.

Personal details

These usually go at the start of your CV. While it's important to include them – you want the employer to know who you are and how they can contact you – they are routine details so shouldn't take up too much space.

> # Curriculum Vitae
>
> Name: Neela Mistry
> Address:
> 33 Union Street,
> Manchester
> M6 3AE
> Phone: 01773 823467
> Email: neela-mistry-33@geemail.com

Setting out your personal details like this takes up a lot of space that you could be using for more significant sections of your CV.

You don't need to use 'Curriculum Vitae' as your heading, or put in the words 'Name', 'Address', 'Phone' or 'Email' – it's obvious what these are!

Neela Mistry

33 Union Street, Manchester M6 3AE
01773 823467 nm33@email.com

Here, by using her name as the heading, putting the address on one line and her phone number and email side by side, Neela gets the same information into only three lines.

Centring the personal details makes a neat heading for your CV.

Profile

A profile (sometimes called a personal statement or a career objective) is a brief summary of your career aim and key selling points that goes at the start of your CV, immediately after your heading and personal details. Think of it as a 'headline' to catch the reader's attention and make them want to find out more.

Don't just give a list of statements with nothing to back them up …

An enthusiastic and highly motivated graduate now looking to enter the business world in a challenging and rewarding position where my intellectual ability, leadership skills, charisma, can-do attitude, ambition and passion to succeed will allow me to thrive.

... but **show** these qualities.

> An enthusiastic and highly motivated graduate now looking to enter the business world. I have strong leadership and persuasive skills and thrive on a challenge, as shown when I set up the university futsal club, recruited and coached members, obtained sponsorship from local businesses and captained the side that won the 2017 national university championships.

A good profile	A poor profile
Is written individually for each position you apply for	Is the same for every CV you write
Is based on the job description and person specification and highlights the skills, experience and/or achievements they set out	Is unfocused and uses clichés and unsubstantiated statements
Is concise – no more than 100 words long at most	Is long and rambling
Takes time and thought	Shows that you haven't put any time and thought into it
Can help to focus your CV by bringing together interesting things about you that may be scattered through different sections of your CV	Is worse than no profile at all. A profile is not compulsory, so if you don't feel that using one will benefit your CV, feel free to leave it out

Adaptable Business and Psychology final-year student seeking to start a career in human resource management. My previous retail management experience has developed strong organisational and communication skills and the ability to multitask while maintaining high standards.

Has a clear career aim and shows how their experience in other areas would be helpful

A creative and professional Media and Communications student with experience of promotional work and social media campaigns for charities and student societies. Seeking an internship in public relations that will use my initiative and communication skills.

Highlights their experience and skills and gives evidence

I am a postgraduate Biodiversity student with a passion for conservation and specific experience in research, data collection and analysis. My practical field work project in Cameroon and my voluntary work experience have involved living in remote areas, learning new skills and techniques quickly and working alongside people from different countries and cultural backgrounds.

Notes general skills, such as teamwork and cultural awareness, as well as subject-specific skills and knowledge

Recently qualified mental health nurse with a keen interest in young people's mental health, particularly anxiety and panic disorders. Completed hospital and community-based placements in CAMHS and another at a university GP practice during my training as well as volunteering with a local teen mental health support group. These have developed my experience of working with clients, families and multidisciplinary teams and my skills in empathy, observation and managing challenging situations.

First-year student seeking part-time retail work alongside my studies. My good GCSE Maths grade and babysitting experience show that I am numerate, reliable and trustworthy.

Education

This section gives a brief summary of your university and secondary education: where you studied and what qualifications you achieved.

If you are still a student, or graduated in the last year or two, your education may be the first main section on your CV, after your personal details and profile (if you use one). If you are applying for positions directly relevant to your degree subject, this lets you show the knowledge and skills you have gained through your studies early on in the CV.

Once you have built up a few years' work experience, or if the experience you have gained through activities outside your studies is likely to be more interesting to employers than your degrees, you will probably want to place your education after your experience.

Example of an education section

List your education in reverse order, with the most recent first

You don't need to list all your modules and projects, but should mention those that relate to the job you're applying for

Use bold text for the names of your university and school. This draws the reader's eye to the key sections

You should give full results for A levels or equivalent qualifications but you may not need to give so much detail for your GCSEs, especially if you took them four or more years ago. Employers usually expect to see your grades for Maths and English and it can also be helpful to give the grades for your best, or most relevant, subjects, but you can summarise the rest to save space

Education

University of Essex, BSc (Hons) Computer Science, 2016 to date

Obtained 62% in my second-year exams: 2:1 predicted in final exams
Modules include:

Software Engineering, Compiling Techniques, Computer Networks
Digital Systems, Operating Systems, Database Systems
Developed programming skills in Java, VB.Net and Python

Project: Development of a Linux-based network system. Achieved 70%

Salford Community College, 2014–2016
A Levels: Mathematics B, Physics C **AS Levels:** Biology C, Chemistry C

St John's School, Manchester, 2009–2014
8 GCSEs at grades A–C including Mathematics (A), English (B) and ICT (A)

Experience

You can put any kind of work-related experience into this section.

You could also use 'Employment', 'Work experience' or 'Career history' as a heading for this section. The last two work well if you don't have much formal paid employment.

If you have plenty of experience you want to include, you could divide this section into 'Relevant' and 'Other' Experience, as in the example below.

Give a brief outline of what you did in each role. You could also say what you learned or what skills you gained through it.

AMS Corner Shop, Norwich Sales Assistant   June–July 2017

- Assisted customers and handled payments in a busy convenience store
- Learned what is involved in running a small business
- Developed communication, numeracy and teamworking skills

Example of an experience section

This CV is targeted on media employers, so this section is headed 'Media experience', which shows immediately that you have experience relevant to the media

Bullets help to make your CV attractive and easy to read. Keep to simple, plain bullets and make sure that you use a consistent bullet style and indentation

Use the names of employers or organisations as subheadings and put them in bold text. You don't need to give their full postal addresses

You can use your 'Other experience' section to show your transferable skills, such as people skills, creativity and responsibility

MEDIA EXPERIENCE
2017–2018 Communications Officer, University of Stirling Students' Union

- Promoted activities, meetings and campaigns through social media, the SU website, radio and print
- Liaised with SU sabbatical officers, university officials and external media

2017–2018 Campus Ambassador for Sports Camps USA

- Organised and publicised meetings and gave presentations
- Provided information for students on summer employment in the USA

OTHER EXPERIENCE
2016–2017 Sales Adviser, Chef Cookware, Stirling (part time)

- Advised customers, gave product demonstrations, handled payments
- Learned about new products and understood customers' needs

Summer 2017 Activity Leader, Camp Koshokona, Wisconsin, USA

- Responsible for looking after a group of children aged 9–13
- Devised creative games and activities and worked with the children to write and perform sketches for the farewell revue

If you have some substantial experience that relates to the post you are now applying for, such as an internship or placement year, you can give more detail about this work and your responsibilities.

June–September 2018 FIDG Bank, London
Internship in Mergers and Acquisitions

Finance employers will know what these mean!

▶ Used Excel for modelling and valuations
▶ Researched deals and companies using a variety of resources including Thomson One and Zephyr
▶ Created an LBO model for a medical diagnostics company
▶ Developed a due diligence template for deal files
▶ Contributed to pitch books and client presentations

*Each of these bullets starts with an **action verb** – see Chapter 10*

Don't give *too* much detail though. Five or six bullet points should be plenty to cover the key points of your experience.

Skills

Although you can use the education, experience and interests sections of your CV to show your skills, you can also include a stand-alone skills section. This draws attention to your key skills.

Skills sections can vary in length and content. They may be just a few lines or may be the main focus of your CV.

Short practical skills section

The most basic skills section is a short list of your practical skills. This may be general, listing skills that may be useful in all kinds of workplaces …

> ▶ **Languages** Good knowledge of French and Spanish
> ▶ **IT** Competent in MS Word, Excel, PowerPoint and MS Access
> ▶ **Driving** Full clean UK driving licence

or it may list the particular skills required in a specialist area of work:

> ▶ **Programming languages:** Java (three years' experience), C++ (proficient), Python and PHP (good working knowledge)
> ▶ **Operating systems:** MS Windows 10, Linux, QNX
> ▶ **Applications:** Dreamweaver CS6, Photoshop

If your course and work or volunteering experience are directly relevant to the position you're applying for, this short outline of your skills may be all that you need. You can focus the rest of your CV on your experience and studies.

If you have a diverse range of experience, or are applying for positions that don't obviously relate to your degree, a more substantial skills section can pull your key skills together and clearly show employers what you have to offer.

Expanded skills section

This section focuses on those transferable skills we looked at on pages 8–9. It needs to be more than just a list, as the only way to prove that you have these skills is to say what you have done that demonstrates them. Write a sentence about each skill that you list.

A Skills section like this will be roughly equal in length to your Education and Experience sections. It is useful to place it before these sections as it sets out your key selling points before going on to give more detail about your studies and other experiences.

SKILLS

Written communication: Wrote articles and features for student publications
Interpersonal skills: Working in customer service roles, I built relationships quickly with people of varied backgrounds and ages
Social media: Ran Facebook, Twitter, Instagram and Snapchat accounts for the Student Union, increasing their following to 75% of the student body
Presentation skills: Visited schools and colleges as a campus ambassador to speak about university and encourage students to apply
Planning and organisation: Managed a busy schedule of part-time work, Student Union and sporting activities alongside my final-year studies
Data handling: Used databases and spreadsheets for course projects

The skills section as the focus of your CV

You could go even further and structure the whole of your CV around your skills. 'Skills' will be the main section of your CV, using the skills needed for the job as subheadings. Under each subheading, give two or three examples that show evidence of this skill. This evidence can come from any area of your life: study, paid employment, volunteering, extracurricular activities or family responsibilities.

Teamwork

- Supervised and managed a team of 12 full and part-time staff
- As a youth club volunteer, I worked with others to plan and deliver activities that would appeal to members while building their skills and confidence
- Worked on three team-based projects a year during my degree, with a new group on each project. Awarded the departmental prize for our final-year project.

Analytical skills

- Analysed sales figures using Excel, and allocated targets to team members
- Used statistical packages to analyse data for psychology projects
- Listened to customers' technical problems and worked with them to devise solutions
- Monitored trends in the consumer electronics industry to anticipate customer demands.

These longer skills sections must focus on the skills needed in this position. Use the job description and person specification to decide which skills to include.

A good skills-focused CV will probably need to be two pages long, which gives you room for around six skills, with examples. The other sections of your CV can be much shorter. You still need to include factual information such as your education, employers and job titles but you don't need to give details of your job roles or activities as these will be covered through your skills examples.

Mature students and career changers often find that this skills-focused approach works much better for them than listing previous jobs. It shows what you **can do** rather than what you **have done** in the past.

Interests

Employers are interested in your interests! You may think of them as 'just hobbies' but employers like to see them in applications for a number of reasons. Your interests can:

❯ **Give evidence of your skills.** This is especially important if you don't yet have much work experience.

My interests include:	This shows that I can:
Competitive sports	Work in a team and handle pressure
Chess, coding or repairing cars	Analyse and solve problems
Playing a musical instrument	Commit to practising and persevere until I reach the desired standard
Acting	Work in a team and meet deadlines
Running a student society	Take the lead and organise other people
Parachuting, potholing or mountaineering	Take risks while being reliable and aware of safety procedures
Blogging, writing short stories, the student newspaper	Write in different styles and make topics interesting

▶ **Show you as an individual,**
giving the employer a real
insight into your personality
and what makes you tick. Your
interests can add sparkle to your
application and, especially if
they are a bit different, help you
to stick in the recruiter's mind.

*A recruiter for an environmental
consultancy looked at the 'Interests'
section of the CV first. If there was
no evidence of outdoor interests such
as sports or mountaineering, the
candidate was rejected as not suitable
for an outdoor role.*

*A law student was applying for training contracts with City solicitors' firms. Like an awful
lot of law students, she had excellent academic grades and had done several work experience
placements in law firms – but she had something different to offer. She loved steam trains
and had volunteered on a heritage railway during the vacations. At every interview she went
to, she was asked about this. It helped her to stand out from all the other candidates and
gave her something she could talk about confidently and enthusiastically at interviews.*

Setting out your CV

▶ **Prove your commitment to an area of work.** If you are sufficiently interested in politics, technology or theatre to spend your spare time doing it, you are showing the motivation to get into it as a career.

> *If you want to train as a teacher, you have to be motivated. If you've coached sports, run a Scouts or Guides group, taught Sunday school or volunteered in a youth club that shows that you enjoy being around children.*

(Recruiter for teacher training courses)

Making your interests section effective

Your interests should say something about you that the reader will find, well, interesting!

Interests: Reading, films, going to the gym, socialising with friends

A list like this doesn't add anything to your CV and could even work against you:

> *'"Socialising with friends" or "spending time with my family" are things that pretty much everybody does — social interactions are part of being a human being. For me, putting these on your CV is pretty uninspiring — you might just as well put "eating and sleeping".'*

(Hospitality recruitment manager)

Don't worry, most people haven't climbed Kilimanjaro or been president of the Student Union and wouldn't dare to audition for *Britain's Got Talent*. You may be too busy studying, working or with your family responsibilities to get deeply involved with clubs or societies.

But, however common your interests may be, they will come over more effectively if you don't just list them but say something about them and what you get out of them.

Interests: I enjoy reading science fiction and fantasy, particularly William Gibson and Pat Cadigan. Many of my friends share this interest and we regularly get together to watch sci-fi films and have lively discussions about the issues they raise. I go to the gym three or four times a week and motivate myself by setting targets to continually improve my performance.

The more you get involved with your interests, the more you can say about them on your CV and the more ways you have to show your skills and enthusiasms. Most universities have a vast range of clubs and societies so do take advantage of these if you can.

As captain of the cricket team, I set a positive example, motivating and coaching players and thinking on my feet when making bowling and field position changes, often in tense situations.

As a volunteer youth worker in Birmingham, I needed energy and imagination to deliver results. I prepared young people for youth parliament, helping to equip them with the skills required to take up their role in society; this included organising a visit to Parliament.

YOUTH CLUB

OPEN

As part of my church choir, I organised a gospel singing night for the university Catholic Society. I planned the food, performances, venue and publicity. Ninety students attended, and we raised £300 for charity.

If you really don't feel that your interests would add anything special to your CV, or you wouldn't feel comfortable talking about your interests at interview, then an interests section isn't compulsory. It's fine to leave it out when you can show your personality and skills through other sections of your CV.

References

Most employers will ask you to give a reference at some stage of the application process, but you don't usually need to give full contact details of your referees on your CV, unless a recruiter specifically asks for these details.

Normally, though, it's fine just to say 'available on request'. If you are really short of space, you could leave out any mention of referees: recruiters know you will provide them if asked!

A good mix is one referee from education (a teacher or university tutor) and one current or previous employer. Try to choose referees who can talk about your personal qualities, rather than just give details of your academic grades or dates of employment. Ask for their permission and give them a copy of your CV or application form.

Most employers won't take up references until they invite you for interview, or maybe even after the interview. When they do, they will most likely contact your referees by phone or email, so make sure that you include these details. It's still useful to give a postal address too, as this helps to confirm the referee's identity.

Referees:

Dr Sara Abrams	Ms Wendy Williams
Senior Lecturer	Store Manager
School of English	Asco plc
University of Medway	Rhes Flaen Retail Park
Rochester	Pontypool
Kent	Gwent
ME7 1QZ	NP4 0BT
s.p.abrams@medway.ac.uk	wendy.j.williams@asco-stores.co.uk
01634 758381	01495 123456

Many careers sites (such as Prospects and TARGETjobs) and recruitment agency sites (such as Reed and GRB) have full example CVs, showing various possible styles and layouts. Take a look at these and think about which model would work best for you.

As well as providing the right information, your CV has to look good. Employers will start to judge it before they have even begun to read it. If it is clearly laid out and easy to read, it will make a positive first impression and give you a strong advantage. If not, it could be rejected without even being read!

Does your CV pass the arm's-length test?

Hold your printed CV at arm's length – far enough away that you cannot actually read the text. What visual impact does it make?

This has too much white space, making it look as though the candidate has little to say

This is too crowded, with too much information in each section. It would take more time to read than most employers are prepared to give

This is clearly set out and the sections are a good length, giving enough detail but not too much

The font you use is part of this visual impact. Choose a font that is clearly readable in print and across different devices. Tahoma and Verdana were both designed for readability on screen. Georgia, Calibri and Arial are also good clear fonts. Use an appropriate size for your font as some take up more space than others. The chart below gives you an idea of what different fonts look like in different sizes.

| Tahoma | 11 point | Georgia | 11 point | Arial | 11 point |
| Verdana | 10 point | Calibri | 12 point | | |

Assessing your CV's visual impact

Do the layout and font make it easy and clear to read?	
Is there enough white space to make the document clear and readable but not so much that the page looks empty?	
Have you used bold headings to signpost the reader to relevant sections?	
Are your headings and fonts consistent throughout?	
Have you used bullet points rather than long paragraphs of text?	
Are the margins too narrow/too wide/just right?	

One side or two?

Some employers specify a one-page CV but most leave the length up to you.

One-page CVs	Two-page CVs	More than two pages
Many employers like these, as they save them time. In some countries, such as the USA, one page is seen as the maximum for an entry-level candidate. They can be harder to write than longer CVs, as every word must count and every piece of information must be relevant.	These are perfectly acceptable for most British and Irish employers. It is better to write a two-side CV than to try to cram too much detail into a single side. If you use two sides, fill as much of the second side as possible. Put the most important information on the first side so that the reader sees it immediately.	These are too long for a student or recent graduate! Unless you are applying for a lectureship or similar academic position (where CVs are longer), employers are unlikely to take the time to read anything more than two sides.

CV checklist

Does your CV cover the following areas?

Targeting	
Focus on a specific job or career area?	
Highlight experience, skills and qualifications that relate to the job description and person specification?	
Have a structure that conveys effectively what you have to offer?	
Personal information	
Include up-to-date and accurate contact details?	
Give a professional image of you (especially your email address!)?	
Profile	
Give concise information, relevant to the position applied for, and make the employer want to read on?	
Education	
List your degree first and then work back?	
Include accurate grades for school, college and university qualifications?	

Work experience	
Give enough information to make your responsibilities clear without going into too much detail?	
Show what skills you gained through this experience?	
Interests	
Make these interesting – not just a list of one-word activities?	
Include them for a reason, showing your motivation, commitment, skills or ability to take responsibility?	
Accuracy	
Have perfect spelling and grammar? (Use a spell-checker to make sure!)	
Have any errors that a spell-checker could have missed? (Double-check it yourself, or get a friend to check, to make sure that it doesn't!)	
Get the dates right and have no unexplained gaps?	

Don't let your email address stop your CV from giving a professional impression of you

Without a cover letter, a CV is incomplete. A letter that says no more than 'Please find attached my CV for the position of ...' is missing an opportunity.

The only times you don't need to send a cover letter with a CV are:

- When an employer specifically says 'no cover letters'
- If you are uploading your CV to attach to an online application form
- When uploading your CV to a recruitment site where it may be seen by many employers.

Application forms are usually complete in themselves and don't need cover letters. Sometimes, though, you may be asked to send or upload one with your application form. If the form only gives you very limited space, you may also want to send or attach a cover letter with it.

What to put in your cover letter

A cover letter is a highly individual document and there is no one way to set it out but the key points to include are as follows.

Introduction:

▶ Give a brief summary of who you are ('a second-year student ...', 'a graduate with six months' experience in ...').

▶ State the job you're applying for – the employer may be recruiting for more than one position! If the job ad has a reference number for this job, quote it in your letter.

▶ Say where you found out about it, for example TARGETjobs, Milkround.com, social media, a local paper or job site. Organisations like to know which of their advertising channels are working successfully.

Why you are the right person for the job:

▶ Using the job description and person specification, say what you can offer in terms of skills, qualifications and experience, and relate these to the competencies that will be required in the job.

▶ You could also describe your motivation here: why you want the job, why you're interested in that type of work and that organisation.

Any other relevant information:

▶ You may, for instance, want to explain poor exam results or any gaps in your career history due to factors such as illness or course changes. Don't go into too much detail and, as far as possible, be positive, for example saying what you have learned from these experiences. You could also use this section to say when you would be available to start work, or for interview.

Conclusion:

▶ Thank the employer and finish with a positive phrase such as 'I look forward to hearing from you'.

Keep your paragraphs brief – seven lines should be the absolute maximum. A cover letter should be no more than one side of A4 paper if printed out.

Base your cover letter on the job ad, job description and/or person specification. Note the key points and think about how you can show that you have what the employer is looking for.

Research Interns

You will be working as part of a team **researching** content (both text and images) for a series of innovative visitor guides to privately owned historic properties. Excellent historical **research, data management and writing skills** are essential, but good **communication skills** are also required as you will be communicating via email and phone with property owners, property managers and public relations teams. You should be able to **manage your own work, meet deadlines and pay close attention to detail**. Apply with CV and letter to henriettacecil@armadabooks.co.uk.

In the extract below, the candidate shows that they have thought about their key experience by using it to give evidence of the skills this employer is looking for. The employer's notes and highlights show that they have made a positive impression!

While at university, I have used my communication skills as secretary of the Fashion Society. As well as publicising events to members through different media, I project-managed a successful fashion show where my responsibilities included contacting retailers by phone and email to persuade them to provide outfits for the show. I coordinated the many different elements of the event while researching for my dissertation and meeting essay deadlines.

Has the right skills and gives evidence for them

Writes well and clearly. Accurate spelling and grammar

I am keen to work for Armada as I have used a number of your publications in my studies and was impressed by their high standards.

Familiar with our products

How to start and end your letter – and how not to

When you know the recipient's name		When you don't know the recipient's name	
Start			
Dear Ms Bloggs	✓	Dear Sir or Madam	✓
Dear Mrs/Miss Bloggs	✗	Dear Human Resources Manager	✓
Dear Lucy Bloggs	✗	Dear Graduate Recruitment Team	✓
Dear Ms Lucy Bloggs	✗	Dear Sirs	✗
Dear Lucy	✗	To whom it may concern	✗
Hi Lucy	✗	Hi	✗
End			
Yours sincerely	✓	Yours faithfully	✓

Phrases such as 'Best wishes' or single words such as 'Yours', 'Sincerely' or 'Cheers' are not appropriate endings for any cover letter.

Sending your CV and cover letter

Even something as simple as how you send these documents can affect the employer's response.

To: recruitmentteam@beyondinfinity.com
From: harry.ling@uni.ac.uk
Subject: CV

Attachment: CV.docx 📎 Cover letter.docx 📎
Please find attached my CV and cover letter for the Aerospace Engineer Summer Internship.
Regards
Harry Ling

Sending your CV and cover letter as an attachment to a basic email such as this is a wasted opportunity. It does the bare minimum but does nothing to encourage the reader to open the attachments.

Using your cover letter as the text of the email grabs attention and makes the reader want to open your CV and find out more about you.

To: recruitmentteam@beyondinfinity.com

From: harry.ling@uni.ac.uk

Subject: CV for Aerospace Engineer Summer Internship

Attachment: Harry Ling CV.docx

Dear Sir or Madam

I am a second-year student of Aerospace Engineering at Brunel University and wish to apply for the Aerospace Engineer Summer Internship advertised on Gradcracker.com.

My course modules have included Aerospace Laboratories, Technical Drawing and Workshop Experience. I achieved a First Class result in my first-year exams.

I am taking a module in aircraft design during my second year and am excited at the possibility of working on the next-generation Aircruiser during my internship.

As a member of the university Rocket Society I have worked in teams on practical challenges to design, build and launch rockets to stringent specifications and have represented the university in national competitions.

I attach my CV and look forward to hearing from you.

Yours faithfully

Harry Ling

If you send your CV and letter by post, use a large envelope so you don't need to fold your documents, and make sure that you attach the right stamp for this size.

A successful cover letter

▶ is targeted on one particular job and employer. Don't try to create a 'template cover letter'; instead, write your letter from scratch for every application
▶ doesn't repeat your CV but complements and expands on it, adding further information and detail and giving an insight into you as an individual
▶ shows your motivation and enthusiasm
▶ answers the questions: 'Why should I choose you? What can you bring to this job?'
▶ is well written. Your cover letter demonstrates your written communication skills and attention to detail: any mistakes in spelling and grammar could mean rejection
▶ makes the employer want to meet you!

You can find full example cover letters on the Prospects and TARGETjobs careers sites.

PART 4

SUCCESSFUL APPLICATION FORMS

Unlike CVs, where you have a lot of flexibility in deciding the style and content, application forms are tightly structured. Employers ask you to answer specific questions and give evidence for particular skills.

You may need to write in a different style too. CVs use short, pithy sentences, lists and bullet points. Application forms often ask you to write paragraphs, but these should still be brief and to the point. In this part of the book, we show you how to write in a concise but lively style that you can use in cover letters as well as application forms.

Forms used by smaller employers may just ask for your personal and educational details and work experience, but big employers usually use more complex forms. Often, you complete the same form for internships, placements and graduate schemes. The most common types of question on these forms are motivational questions and competency questions:

▶ **Competency questions** seek to find out **if you can do the job**: whether you have the practical skills and competencies set out in the job description.
▶ **Motivational questions** seek to find out **why you want the job**: whether you also have the transferable skills and personal qualities set out in the person specification.

Some forms use other types of questions, including questions about your **strengths**, your **interests** or just **any other information**. These last two are often used by smaller employers and give you a chance to stand out and show something of your personality, particularly if your previous work experience is limited. Other employers may use **situational judgement questions** or **psychometric/personality tests**.

Competency questions

These ask you to provide evidence of skills that are used in the job, typically through questions such as:

> Give an example of a time when you have 'gone the extra mile' to provide excellent customer service.

> Describe a situation or problem that required you to think differently and come up with a creative solution.

> Tell us about a time when you worked as part of a team and outline the skills you used to influence the outputs of that team.

> When did you have to prioritise a number of different tasks at the same time?

Start by brainstorming examples you could use. These could come from any part of your life:

- vacation or part-time work
- university clubs and societies
- voluntary work
- study at school or university
- holidays and travel or personal and family experiences.

Give recent and relevant examples and make sure they are not all from study or the same work experience.

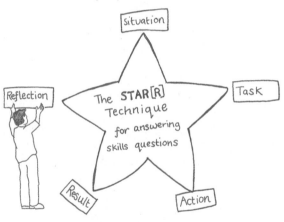

Compose a paragraph or so for each situation. This should be set out as a brief story that covers the background to the situation, says what you did and what the outcome was. Use the STAR format to structure your answer.

STAR stands for Situation, Task, Action and Result. Sometimes Reflection is added to these.

	Give an example of a time when you have 'gone the extra mile' to provide excellent customer service.	
S T	**The SITUATION and TASK form the introduction:** ▶ Describe the situation and the specific task you were faced with: when, where, with whom? ▶ What did you set out to achieve? ▶ Was there a timescale?	*(SITUATION) I was working as a sales assistant (TASK) when a customer phoned to ask if a purse had been left in the store.*
A	**The ACTION forms the body and is the longest part of your answer:** ▶ What action did you take? Detail what you actually did. What were the day-to-day tasks? What was your approach to achieving it? ▶ Why did you adopt this approach? How and why were decisions made? How did you convince others to buy into your change or idea? ▶ What obstacles did you have to overcome and how did you do this?	*(ACTION) I went round the store asking at all the counters and then looked in the changing rooms, where I found the purse on the floor. I gave it to the manager and we looked in the purse to confirm the customer's identity and address. She lived quite close to me so, when I phoned her to tell her that the purse had been found, I offered to deliver it to her after work to save her getting a bus into town again.*

R	**The RESULT** Give a brief conclusion showing if the task was a success. What positive impact did your actions have? What changed as a result of your efforts? A quantified result, involving numbers, gives a stronger impression of your achievement; e.g. 'during my leadership, membership rose by a third', 'we raised £200 for charity', 'my marks improved from 55% to 65%'.	*(RESULT) She was delighted and wrote to the store manager saying that I deserved an Employee of the Month award.*
R	You can also add **REFLECTION** – what you learned and, if appropriate, what you might do differently if a similar situation occurred again.	*This showed me how, even in a big company, customers still appreciate the personal touch.*

Think about what the employer wants to see and whether your answer is giving them this.

The focus should be on **you** – even if the situation involved a group, show what your specific role was in achieving the desired result.

If it was a group task, what was your specific contribution and role? Sometimes, students focus on what the group did without mentioning their own contribution. How were the individuals in the team different? What challenges did you face working with them? How did you keep everyone focused and motivated to achieve the goal?

Below are two answers to the question, **Give an example of a time when you have worked in a team to achieve a goal**, with an employer's responses:

That should have capital Ps

Who is 'we'?

In my second year I had to do a group project as part of my Business module. We researched a company, carried out a SWOT analysis and presented our findings. This required good organisational and communication skills to meet the deadline. We used powerpoint for the presentation and all of us took turns to speak. The project achieved a 2.1 grade, which was a positive outcome as we all had a lot of other assignments at that time so we had to work under pressure to meet the deadline.

This is a bit rambling and repetitive

How did you show these?

Yes, but what did YOU do?

As part of my Business module I took part in a mock consultancy project. We worked in teams of four to research a company, carry out a SWOT analysis and present our recommendations. Our team made a collective decision on which company to use and agreed to divide up the analysis between us. My responsibility was to research the 'threats' aspect and I also arranged weekly meetings to coordinate our work and discuss the next stage. I also introduced the final PowerPoint presentation, where each of us spoke on our individual research. The project achieved a 2.1 grade.

You could also add REFLECTION on what you learned from this experience, what you did well and what not so well. For example:

'I learned from this project that sharing information and keeping track of everybody's work is essential. On my next project I set up a shared folder for this purpose, which worked very successfully.'

Employers expect graduates to be able to reflect and learn from their experiences, which is why they ask questions about your weaknesses at interview: they are finding out if you learn and grow from your mistakes and failures or keep repeating the same old mistakes.

Motivational questions

These ask why you want to work for that employer and in that job:

> What attracted you to your chosen business area within Unilever?

> What attracted you to apply for the Unilever placement programme?

> What is it about working for Monsoon that interests you?

> Give us two good reasons why you would like to work for Nando's.

> What do you understand the role of an international commercial lawyer to be and why are you pursuing that role?

If you can show that you really are keen to work for the organisation and have an understanding of what you'll be doing in this role, it will reassure them that you will work with enthusiasm.

The selector will look for evidence that you've analysed your skills, qualities and experience and matched these carefully with those required. This will help you to talk about what you can do for the company rather than what they can do for you. Find something distinctive to say about yourself, not just things many other interviewees might say, such as 'I'm a good communicator' or 'I work well in a team'.

Show knowledge of the company, the job and why it's right for you. Don't quote their website back at them. Instead, show why you feel that you'll fit the organisation well. Find things the employer is proud of: their clients, products, successes, environmental policies or training.

> Nobody would apply to a 'disreputable' organisation, would they?

What do you think of this answer?

I have chosen to apply to your company because it is a highly reputable organisation, which offers challenging opportunities in a friendly and supportive environment. The company's graduate training programme is well respected and would be an excellent start to my career.

> Using our name here would be nice – does he even know it?

> Well, we like to think so but what makes him say that?

Other things to avoid are salary or perks, trying to fake a passion for the business, giving bland answers, such as 'It seems a great place to work', or giving answers that suggest you are not taking the application seriously:

'My lifelong love of chocolate biscuits is the main reason for my interest in the company.'

This is a much better answer:

He shows a genuine reason for choosing us

Positive attitude

The relatively small intake of 10 graduates makes Company X particularly appealing to me. I want to work in an environment where I can make a real contribution at an early stage and will not simply be a small cog in a large machine. I was also interested to read that Company X was awarded the top 3-star rating in the 'Best Companies to Work For' list, which encourages me to believe that it would offer me high-quality training.

He's done some in-depth research on us

Situational judgement questions

These assess your understanding of and/or suitability for the job. They aim to be fair and open without any bias towards a particular gender, ethnic or social background. Because they are based on real-life situations related to the job and the employer, they are a good predictor of performance.

Researching the job and the employer will help you to understand the type of person they are looking for, the culture of the organisation and the situations you may encounter in the job.

Don't try to fake it though – be yourself! If you feel you have to put on an act to get this job, is it really the right one for you?

These questions are increasingly used by graduate recruiters, including major energy, technology and finance employers and the Civil Service. One supermarket uses 'situational judgement' questions for customer service assistant roles, such as:

You are serving at the checkout but the store is very quiet at the moment and there are no customers waiting to be served at your checkout. A customer asks you where they can find a particular item. Would you:

A. Leave your checkout and take the customer to the section where the item is shelved.

This shows good customer service, but the supermarket might have a policy on not leaving your checkout during a shift

B. Give the customer directions to the aisle where they can find the item.

This would help the customer to some extent but does not show such good customer service as A

C. Call a colleague who is refilling shelves nearby and ask them to show the customer to the section where the item is shelved.

This would provide more positive help to the customer than option B without you leaving the checkout, so would be ranked as 'most effective'

D. Leave your checkout, take the customer to the section where the item is shelved and then take the opportunity to slip off for a quick break while the store is quiet.

This would help this particular customer but does not show a very positive or motivated attitude on your part, so would definitely be 'least effective'

Psychometric tests

Online application forms may include tests – most often verbal and numerical reasoning – but technology and engineering companies may also use spatial reasoning tests, while some large law and finance firms use critical thinking tests.

Don't panic! There are many resources to help you to practise these tests and become familiar with the type of questions and test structure, either online or through your university careers service. This practice will make the tests less daunting and improve your performance.

- SHL practice tests, www.cebglobal.com/shldirect/en/practice-tests
- Prospects, www.prospects.ac.uk/interview_tips_psychometric_tests.htm
- TARGETjobs, http://targetjobs.co.uk/careers-advice/psychometric-tests
- Assessment Day, www.assessmentday.co.uk

Whether made by CV and cover letter or by application form, your application is not just about what you say. How you say it is equally important. However outstanding you are as a candidate, if your application is hard to read an employer will not read it! Your use of language and how you organise and present what you have to say are significant.

Be clear and concise

You may only have 150 words to write an answer to a question on an application form and CVs should not be more than two pages long, so, if in doubt, cut it out. Avoid clichés. Recruiters aren't impressed by formal, long-winded language and jargon: straightforward, natural writing is always preferred.

Jargon, waffle and clichés	Clear and effective
Within the workplace	At work
I am a person who thinks outside the box	I am a creative thinker
Responsible for reaching out to clients	Responsible for contacting clients
Going forward on my career journey …	In future …
Furthermore, I was awarded a prize …	I was also awarded a prize …

Applicant 1	Applicant 2
I'm a dynamic, passionate and motivated team player with a proven track record and a unique strategic vision allowing me to increase leverage by paradigm shifts to push the envelope forward.	*I have developed strong organisational and problem-solving skills through my involvement with Rag fundraising and promotional work. I successfully combined my studies with these other commitments, showing myself to be self-motivated and a good time manager.*
Selector's comments	
This answer gives no evidence and is full of jargon.	This applicant uses more straightforward language and backs up their claims with evidence.

Structure your paragraphs

Paragraphs are not just for cover letters: if you have more than 100 words to answer a question on an application form, breaking your answer into short paragraphs will make it easier to read.

Whether in a CV, a cover letter or an application form, each paragraph should:

▶ introduce an idea

▶ develop it briefly

▶ conclude it or link to the next paragraph.

Express the main idea, show your evidence, show what you learned or achieved, as shown in the answer below.

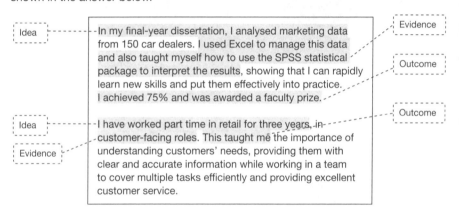

Idea

Evidence

Outcome

Outcome

Idea

Evidence

In my final-year dissertation, I analysed marketing data from 150 car dealers. I used Excel to manage this data and also taught myself how to use the SPSS statistical package to interpret the results, showing that I can rapidly learn new skills and put them effectively into practice. I achieved 75% and was awarded a faculty prize.

I have worked part time in retail for three years, in customer-facing roles. This taught me the importance of understanding customers' needs, providing them with clear and accurate information while working in a team to cover multiple tasks efficiently and providing excellent customer service.

Brilliant writing tips for students in this series has more advice on structuring your paragraphs and sentences and the tricky area of punctuation.

Action words: bring your application to life

Action words, usually verbs, show clearly what you have done. They demonstrate your skills in terms that employers can relate to. Using them in your applications helps you to come across as motivated and enthusiastic.

Passive expressions such as 'were interviewed' make the answer dull and impersonal

Using 'I' focuses it on you and what you achieved

Which of these statements gives the more positive impression of this applicant?

'For my final-year project, I had to do a survey of patients' attitudes to healthcare services for the elderly. Patients were interviewed both in hospital and in their homes and data collected was entered on a database. This project was finished on time and was awarded a 2.1 grade.'	*'I devised and prepared a survey of elderly patients' attitudes to healthcare services as my final-year project. I interviewed 70 patients and obtained a substantial amount of data. I then created a database to analyse and interpret this material. I completed this project three weeks ahead of schedule and achieved a 2.1 grade.'*

Avoid the phrase 'I had to ...' – it sounds like something you didn't want to do!

Lots of action words!

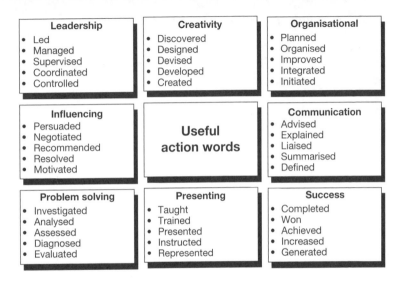

Leadership	**Creativity**	**Organisational**
• Led • Managed • Supervised • Coordinated • Controlled	• Discovered • Designed • Devised • Developed • Created	• Planned • Organised • Improved • Integrated • Initiated
Influencing	**Useful action words**	**Communication**
• Persuaded • Negotiated • Recommended • Resolved • Motivated		• Advised • Explained • Liaised • Summarised • Defined
Problem solving	**Presenting**	**Success**
• Investigated • Analysed • Assessed • Diagnosed • Evaluated	• Taught • Trained • Presented • Instructed • Represented	• Completed • Won • Achieved • Increased • Generated

Check your spelling

Make sure that your application is correctly spelt. This advice may seem obvious, but several surveys have shown that over half of graduate CVs and application forms contain spelling mistakes. These suggest that you are either careless, lacking in written communication skills or just not bothered about your application – any of which give the employer a reason to reject your application.

Don't just rely on your spell-checker but proofread your application carefully. Spell-checkers won't pick up on real words in the wrong context, such as:

'In my spare time, I enjoy hiding my horse.'

Take CARE over your applications

Improve your chances of making your application successful by remembering that it should be:

Clear   in layout, structure and wording

Accurate   in content and spelling

Relevant   to that job and that employer

Enthusiastic   making the effort to do all the above will go a long way towards showing your enthusiasm and motivation

---

No matter how good your application form or CV, it won't lead directly to a job or placement offer: it's just the first step towards getting this offer. You will have to attend interviews and perhaps an assessment day. You may make several applications before you are invited to an interview, so learning how to accept rejection will help you to develop resilience. Once you have got your first job, it's wise to think about how to develop your career.

Congratulations! If you have been offered an interview, you are probably in the top 20% of candidates, so have already done well.

In smaller organisations, you may only have one interview before the employer makes their decision. Larger employers may have several stages, including telephone interviews, aptitude tests and an assessment centre.

Preparation

Preparation (or lack of it!) is the reason many people succeed or fail at interviews. Much of this preparation has been covered in this book, such as carefully researching the employer, job and industry. Knowing how to research jobs will also help to answer interview questions on why you want the job.

Key steps in the interview process

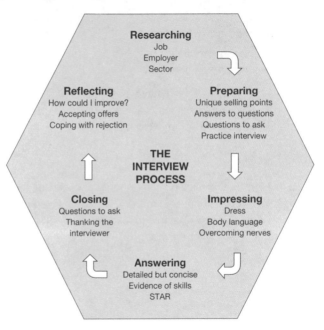

Researching
Job
Employer
Sector

Reflecting
How could I improve?
Accepting offers
Coping with rejection

Preparing
Unique selling points
Answers to questions
Questions to ask
Practice interview

**THE
INTERVIEW
PROCESS**

Closing
Questions to ask
Thanking the
interviewer

Impressing
Dress
Body language
Overcoming nerves

Answering
Detailed but concise
Evidence of skills
STAR

The interview iceberg

Most interview success comes from what can't be seen during the interview. Like an iceberg, it's the hidden part that has the most impact: the preparation you do beforehand.

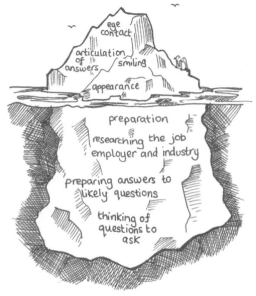

Keep a copy of your application and, before you go to interview, reread it as if you were the interviewer. Think about:

▶ If I was the interviewer, how might I use the application to decide questions to ask?

▶ What parts of my application are most important for this job?

▶ What are my weak points? What parts of my application would I rather not be asked about? (Employers may home in on these areas, so prepare answers in advance.)

Common types of interview question		
Question type	Comments	Example
Open	Can't be answered with just 'yes' or 'no'	*Why do you want this job?*
Closed/leading	Can be answered with just 'yes' or 'no'	*You're bad at maths?*
Forced choice	Force you to choose an answer	*Are you a leader or a follower?*
Competency	Asks for evidence of skills in the job	*Describe a time when you worked in a team*
Motivational	Check you've researched the job	*Who are our competitors?*
Biographical	Based on your CV	*Tell me about your interest in mountaineering*
Ethical	Test honesty and integrity	*Is honesty always the best policy?*
Technical	Technical and scientific questions	*How would you synthesise DNA?*

Cultural fit	Do you fit the organisation's culture?	*How do you feel about working long hours?*
Strengths-based	Focus on your strengths	*What do you learn quickly?*
Hypothetical	'What if …' questions	*If you were a dog, what type would you be?*
Puzzle	Case studies, logic puzzles or brain teasers	*How many buses are there in England?* *Why don't polar bears eat penguins?*

Competency interviews

The skills analysis that you've covered in this book will have prepared you for competency interviews, as the same STAR approach can be used to answer these questions at interview.

You will already have prepared answers to many of the common competency questions, such as: 'Give an example of when you worked effectively in a team.' You can use these answers at interview. Sometimes, an interviewer may ask for elaboration of the answers you gave on the application form or probe your answers, so be prepared for this.

Many interview questions are based on the **job description** and **person specification**. If the person specification requires candidates to be able to achieve targets within agreed timescales, then one question might be: 'Give an example of where you had to achieve targets to tight deadlines.'

Competency interviews are still the most common type of graduate interview, but **strengths-based interviews** are becoming increasingly common. The strengths section of this book on the following pages will help you prepare for these.

You will also normally be expected to ask questions at interview: interviews are a two-way process! Good questions may come from your research into the job and the organisation, on training you might receive and on career development, such as:

▶ Could you tell me about your training programme?
▶ What support would I get for professional development?
▶ How would my performance be appraised during my internship?
▶ What would be the main priorities in my first year?
▶ What kind of career paths have other graduates taken?
▶ How much discretion would there be for me to make my own decisions?
▶ How do you see this role developing?
▶ How would you see the company developing in future?

Write down three questions you could ask below
Show your questions to a friend to get their views on these.

Strengths interviews

Strengths questions are a form of motivational question: they aim to find out what interests you. Competency questions ask **what you can do** (your skills), whereas strengths questions find out **what you enjoy doing**. Strengths-based interviews are becoming increasingly common. Recruiters use the strengths approach as they feel that this results in fewer pre-prepared answers and a more genuine insight into candidates.

Strengths are natural aptitudes such as analysing, organising and working with others. Candidates who are asked questions about their strengths tend to enjoy the interview more and perform better. By matching your strengths to the role, you are likely to find one you enjoy rather than just one you are capable of doing. This will help your application too, as when writing about their strengths, candidates show more passion and come across as more genuine.

Think about what you enjoy doing, such as your hobbies, and be open: don't try to be something you're not. Think of things you are proud to have done. Be honest about what tasks you don't enjoy and think about how your preferences might fit with the organisation's culture and requirements.

Some typical strengths questions asked at interview

Advanced strengths questions put you on the spot and appear to be forcing you to choose from several alternatives. Consider which attribute would be more needed in the job. If you're asked, 'Do you prefer to work on your own or in a team?', don't imply that you are capable of one but not the other; instead, say that the role will dictate which aspect should take precedence. Programmers may spend much time working on their own, whereas for a marketing role, you might emphasise teamwork skills.

▶ Do you prefer to start things or to finish them?
▶ Do you prefer to work in a team or on your own?
▶ Are you spontaneous or organised?
▶ Do you prefer to be right or to be liked?
▶ Would you rather know a lot about a little or a little about a lot?

Do you prefer to lead or to follow?

Both can have positive and negative aspects. If you say you're a leader, you may be perceived as someone who always wants their own way, but if you say you're a follower, you may be seen as someone who can't lead or think for yourself. For a management role, construct your answer to show leadership, whereas for a technical specialist role, it's fine to say you are more of a follower.

Example answer

'I prefer a leadership role as I like to drive things forward, but I do understand that there are times when you have to take a background role and pull together as a team member. When I start work, I will have much to learn and will need to take instruction from those with more experience, but I hope to quickly move into a role where I can use my initiative.'

Interview checklist

- **Dress smartly**: this will boost your confidence.
- **Arrive about 15 minutes before the interview** to give yourself time to find the room and to relax before you are called in.
- **Remind yourself of your good points** to boost your confidence.
- **Be friendly to everyone** you meet: the receptionist is often asked what impression the interviewee made.
- **Make eye contact** with the interviewer, smile and give a firm handshake as the first few minutes are vital.
- **Careful preparation can minimise nerves**, but remember that the interviewer will expect you to be a little nervous.

12 After your interview

Make a note of what went well, or not so well, while the interview is fresh in your mind and analyse your performance. This will help with future interviews.

How well did you answer the interviewer's questions?
Write below any you feel that you answered poorly. Think how you might improve your answer next time. Sometimes, if you are nervous, you may not answer a question well even when you know what you should say! Practice can help with this.

Did you have a good rapport with the interviewer?
Sometimes, if an interview went badly, it could just be a difference in personalities.
Interviewers are human beings too, so don't take this type of difficulty personally.

Were there any questions you found hard to answer? Could you have dealt with them better if you had done more research on the company, job or industry?

What questions did you ask the interviewer? Could you improve on them?

Keeping track

Keep track of your applications and their progress. A database or spreadsheet makes this easy.

Vacancy	Employer	Reference	Date sent	Response received	Comments/ notes
PR Assistant	Viaduct	V2035	18 April	18 April	Rejected
Communications Assistant	Wildlife Protection Trust	-	19 April		Follow up if no response received by 4 May
Trainee Press Officer	Octan	CMD 231/18	21 April	27 April	Telephone interview arranged 3 May, 10.30 am

If you haven't heard back about a job you've applied to after a couple of weeks, it's worth emailing to check what's happening: the employer might be encouraged by your interest.

What if you aren't successful at first?

Rejection is a normal part of the application process: on average, only around 10% of applicants will be offered an interview. Don't take rejection personally, as an unsuccessful application may not be a poor application. You may simply have come up against a lot of high-quality applications.

Review your strategy regularly – not only your application strategy but also your job search and career strategies. Are you using the most appropriate vacancy sources? Are there alternative roles you could apply for? For example, competition for marketing jobs can be intense, but sales roles, which can be a stepping stone into marketing, are easier to obtain. When searching vacancy sites, you may stumble across appealing roles that you didn't know existed, so pursue any such opportunities.

Get help from your university careers service. They work with students and recent graduates to critique your applications, help you to review your strategy and advise on career choice and job sources.

Quality Make sure your CV, letters and application forms are of top quality	**Set yourself goals** Develop an action plan and support network of friends and family	**Stay positive** Job hunting is a series of no's followed by one YES!
Start a course e.g. in business or IT at a local college or online	**How to improve your chances of success**	**Be flexible** About job type & location. Consider casual work
Develop your skills e.g. computing, languages or driving	**Follow enthusiasms** Take up a new hobby, or do voluntary work to build skills	**Keep healthy** Exercise, eat healthily & get some sleep!

Keep motivated. If you are persistent, you'll eventually succeed. Remember that the only guaranteed way not to get a job is not to apply for it!

'Success is going from failure to failure without losing your enthusiasm.'
(Abraham Lincoln)

The key stages in your job hunting journey

PART 1 WHO ARE YOU?
Think about your positive qualities and what evidence you can give of these to the employer

PART 2 RESEARCH
Research the job, employer and sector

PART 3 NETWORKING
Find people who can give you advice and insights

PART 6 APPLICATION FORMS

Read through the questions carefully, and start preparing your answers

Answer the question asked! Check if there is a word limit for answers

PARTS 4 and 5 CVs and COVERING LETTERS

Target the job

Choose a style that works for you

Check for spelling
and other mistakes

Keep a copy of your applications:
you may be able to re-edit content
for other applications

Send it off! Keep track of
all your applications:
note the date sent

PART 7 INTERVIEWS
Preparation is key...

HOORAY: JOB OFFER!

REJECTION!
This is a normal
part of the process
so don't take it
personally: keep your
spirits up and try
again!

Keep developing your career

Your first job, internship or placement is just the start of your career journey and it will lead to others. A LinkedIn study in 2016 found that graduates typically changed jobs between two and four times in the first five years after graduation.

Take stock of yourself and where you are and review your CV regularly. This will help you to measure your career progress and pinpoint attributes you need to develop to move forward, which will be useful at workplace appraisals. Keeping your CV up to date means that you are always prepared if you decide to make an application at short notice.

The skills you've learned throughout this book, such as analysing yourself, writing succinctly and putting across a persuasive argument, will not only help you to make successful applications but also to find success and satisfaction in your career. Together with those skills you have gained throughout your studies, they will stand you in good stead throughout your working life.

Good luck with your applications and on your career journey!

References

Berger G (2016) *Will this year's college grads job-hop more than previous grads?*, https://blog.linkedin.com/2016/04/12/will-this-year_s-college-grads-job-hop-more-than-previous-grads

Copus J (2009) *Brilliant writing tips for students*. London: Red Globe Press.

Godfrey J (2016) *Writing for university,* 2nd edn. London: Red Globe Press.

High Fliers Research (2017) *The graduate market in 2017,* www.highfliers.co.uk

Holland JL (1997) *Making vocational choices: a theory of vocational personalities and work environments,* 3rd edn. Odessa, FL: Psychological Assessment Resources.

Salm L (2017) *70% of employers are snooping candidates' social media profiles,* www.careerbuilder.com/advice/social-media-survey-2017

Turban DB, Stevens CK and Lee FK (2009) 'Effects of conscientiousness and extraversion on new labor market entrants' job search: the mediating role of metacognitive activities and positive emotions'. *Personnel Psychology*, 62, 553–73.

University of Kent Careers and Employability Service (2014) *The creative career search,* www.kent.ac.uk/ces/publications.html

Williams K (2014) *Getting critical,* 2nd edn. London: Red Globe Press.

Williams K (2018) *Planning your dissertation,* 2nd edn. London: Red Globe Press.

Williams K, Woolliams M and Spiro J (2012) *Reflective writing*. London: Red Globe Press.

123test, www.123test.com
Free career and personality tests.

Glassdoor, www.glassdoor.co.uk
Reviews of organisations and their interview processes.

Graduate Recruitment Bureau (2018) *Graduate CV,* www.grb.uk.com/careers-advice/graduate-cv

Leonard I (2015) *Don't improve … in-prove: A LinkedIn guide for students by students.* www.birmingham.ac.uk/Documents/alumni/graduatecareers/linkedIn-guide.pdf

Milkround, www.milkround.com
Graduate jobs, internships, employers, careers advice and a section for school and college leavers.

Prospects, www.prospects.ac.uk
Extensive graduate careers website covering job profiles, careers advice, vacancies for graduate jobs, placements and internships, and advice on applications and

interviews. The Career Planner section, www.prospects.ac.uk/planner, will help you to match your skills and personality to over 400 job profiles and get detailed information about these jobs.

Rate My Placement, www.ratemyplacement.co.uk
Focuses on placements and internships, with feedback from previous students and a blog that includes advice on applications.

Reed.co.uk, *CV templates,* www.reed.co.uk/career-advice/cvs/cv-templates

Rook S (2013) *The graduate career guidebook: advice for students and graduates on careers options, jobs, volunteering, applications, interviews and self-employment.* London: Red Globe Press.

TARGETjobs http://targetjobs.co.uk
Graduate jobs, placements, internships, career sectors, employers, careers advice (covering many of the topics in this book) and careers events.

Woodcock B (2016) *Excel at graduate interviews: how to make the best impression with recruiters.* London: Red Globe Press.

Woodcock B and Keaveney J (2017) *Graduate CVs and covering letters.* London: Red Globe Press.

Index